Improvising Memory

Improvising Memory

Milorad Krystanovich

ISBN: 978-0-9560559-9-6

Copyright © Milorad Krystanovich 2010
Foreword © David Hart 2010
Cover image: *Directing Sunlight* © Milorad Krystanovich
Author Photograph: © Jane Commane

All rights reserved. No part of this work may be reproduced, stored or transmitted in any form or by any means, graphic, electronic, recorded or mechanical, without the prior written permission of the publisher.

Milorad Krystanovich has asserted his right under Section 77 of the Copyright, Designs and Patents Act 1988 to be identified as the author of this work.

First published April 2010 by:

Nine Arches Press
Great Central Studios
92 Lower Hillmorton Rd
Rugby
Warwickshire
CV21 3TF

www.ninearchespress.com

Printed in Britain by:
MPG Biddles Ltd
24 Rollesby Road
Hardwick Industrial Estate
King's Lynn
Norfolk
PE30 4LS

Improvising Memory

Milorad Krystanovich

Nine
Arches
Press

Milorad Krystanovich was born in Croatia and has lived in Birmingham since 1992. He studied Creative Writing at the University of Birmingham and is a member of Writers Without Borders, Cannon Poets and the Society of Children's Book Writers & Illustrators. Milorad works as a language teacher at the Brasshouse Centre in Birmingham. *Improvising Memory* is his sixth poetry collection, and follows on from *The Yasen Tree* (Heaventree Press, 2007).

Neither do men light a candle,
and put it under a bushel,
but on a candlestick;
and it giveth light unto all
that are in the house.

MATTHEW V.15

**Dedicated to my father
Dušan Krstanović
1926 – 2009**

ACKNOWLEDGEMENTS

I am grateful to Cathy Perry, Martin Underwood, Jane Commane, Matt Nunn and David Hart who supported me in bringing out this collection. And to the people who cared and prayed for me.

The poem below is dedicated to all of you.

Directing Sunlight
(The title of my photo from this book cover)

To preserve the lichens of time
found marked on the places
waiting for daylight in the picture
as if exposed on my window-sill,

to have the exhibition of dreams
presented as poems in a book –
I conduct an empty glass vase
to become less empty of rainwater

and improvise it in the poetry gallery.

CONTENTS

FOREWORD   11

INSIDE OUT-CASTING
Telepathic Relief   17
Inside Out-casting   18
Soon   19
Presence   20
Turning   21

SILENT INHERITANCE
Out of Darkrooms   25
Hibernation Cushion   26
Magic Lantern   27
Celluloid Collection   28
Non-communicators   29
Silent Inheritance   30
Removing the Inner-stone   31
In-earth   32
Outside the Paradox   33
Dream Gap   34
Kinetic Construction   35

IMPROVISING MEMORY
Today   39
Love Collocation   40
Improvising Memory   41
No Difference   42
Beyond the Singer   43
Hermitage   44
Tomorrow   45
Two Pretenders   46
Love's Enthusiast   47
Escaping Emptiness   48
Entitled   49

FUTURE FORGOTTEN

Guidance	53
Picture Study	54
Petrified Duet	55
Through the Media of a Moment	56
Into the Reflection	57
Spirit Maturation	58
Attachment	59
Future Forgotten	60
Observation Window	61
Grasping for the Surface	62
Degree of Vacuum	63
Dual Projection	64

FINDING DARKROOM PRINTS

The Imprint of Three Seconds	67
Tepid Support	68
Blossom Rain	69
Joined-up Writing	70
Tethered to Home	71
Now	72
Fading Darkroom Prints	73
Runners from Each Other	74
Rebuilding Warmth	75
Destined	76

DOUBLE IDENTITY

Non-composure	79
Crestfallen Diver	80
Double Identity	81
Two Figures	82
Pining for a Close-up	83
Two Hurts	84
Not an Interpolation	85
Variant Evidence	86

Mourner's Tribute	87
Expiry	88
Dancing Music	89

BLANKETED

Late Honeymoon	93
Crossover	94
Sleep Advantage	95
Synchronicity	96
Silver Winter	97
Continuity	99
Holiday House	100
Still	101
Hunter	102
Anti-burial	103
Blanketed	104

EDITING THE SILENCE FROM THE PHOTOGRAPHS

Inconsistent	107
Retaining	108
Rorschach Test	110

FOREWORD

This book seems to mark a moment for taking stock. It has long puzzled me how we live 24 hours a day for (to date) however many years, but that if asked for a biographical note and are told *in no more that 200 words, please*, we do it. We live the long haul or the merry dance and then sum it up in a paragraph.

Or it might be put like this, for better or worse (and probably we never know) we exist in the terms of other people's conversations about us. We think we have a life of years, when who we are is ten minutes when two friends (or not) meet by chance on a bus.

Or we are our markers. For some reason or another we are listed, our name is in the records, and look, here's a photo. When was that? Don't know, I remember him younger.

Or, *here's one of his poems*. Here's a book of them. So *this* tells us who he is? This is him present and correct, this explains him?

It would not best please a journalist who came with pad and shorthand to record an interview, to be given the book and told, 'This is it, this is me'.

Milorad's first book, after coming to Birmingham from Croatia in 1992 without fluent English, was *Easel And Ashes* (Writers Without Borders, 2000), in Serbo-Croat with English translations, for which Cathy Perry then and later, while herself knowing no Serbo-Croat, was important in his making the transition between the languages. Jonathan Davidson in his Introduction said that "although Milorad's personal history haunts the work this is not just autobiography. Its aims are higher – it is poetry written with a genuine desire to understand, to communicate and to commemorate."

A few of the poems from that first book with a few new ones were included (in Serbo-Croat and English) in the anthology, *Griot*, 2001, edited by Kampta Karran and Cathy Perry, and it is worth noting that the publisher of this, too, was Writers Without Borders, a boundary-crossing group of not a little significance in the Birmingham cultural mix.

The Language of Wounds (WWB), of his own newly English poems, not from Serbo-Croat, followed in 2002. John Alcock in his Introduction said, "At once we can gauge the increase in fluency and command which these poems reveal. In Milorad's case, the 'frontiers of writing' were there to be crossed."

In her Introduction to his next book, *Where Spirits Touch* (WWB, 2004), Brenda Parker wrote, "Milorad has a deep sense of the inextricable closeness of the two [language and experience], and he explores in his poems the chasm created when they are ripped apart."

There is a more complex history in this short survey of his deployment of languages than I can account for: the next book returned to both English and Croatian. *Four Horizons/Cetiri Vidika* (Heaventree, 2005) was in English on the left side of each double page, with as it were a return of the Croatian on the right, as if the English had come first. This book had no introduction.

The latest book prior to this new one, was (in English with no Croatian), *The Yasen Tree* (Heaventree, 2007). In my own Foreword to that book I ventured the thought that Milorad "won't become a Brummie poet but is likely to become in practice and recognition a significant European one." I remain of this opinion. In her review of the book in the final issue of *Raw Edge Magazine*, Julie Boden found there "a confident unEnglish in English".

I have no direct knowledge of Croatia, but my sense of it does not include a Birmingham-type city there at all; nor do these poems conjure the Birmingham I know; something else is going on here. If I may interpolate my own experience, my poems find the Welsh sea willynilly, they find boats, gulls, hills, there is the persistent presence of a desolate hut; I am after 40 years almost beginning to acknowledge I am a Birmingham poet; without the *Cymraeg* never truly a Welsh one.

In this subtle book, full of verbal, atmospheric, relational surprises, there is shadowy light, the moods of weather, light and dark, day and night, of moonlight, of sea, a beach, between waking and dusk, of dreams and day dreams; there is bird, flight, wings, 'wingfriend', there is un-named 'her' and 'his', 'me' and 'you'. One finds mixing even within single metaphor-making sets of lines the abstract notion and the everyday.

I have found myself thinking these poems are in a condition of unstable translation, but not with any notion of their inadequacy or secondariness, on the contrary, only that they are finely balanced in Milorad's catching of them, in their fragile and surprising making.

My hunch is, that in Milorad's cultural past and memory, there is an unEnglish Central European working with the surreal, the imagist, expressionist (I attach mere labels), in poetry parallel to movements in the visual arts. One might speak of the dream/nightmare world of the wide-awake poet.

To give the book some context in time and space, the poems were written in Birmingham during the few years prior to mid-May 2009, when they were brought together for publication. The book is innocent of what was to happen shortly afterwards, when Milorad was diagnosed with a brain tumour. The poems relate to, are the signs of, are the insights, memories, people he met, was with, during that previous time.

After almost a year of medical treatment, Milorad remains delightfully present, not yet certain of the eventual outcome, not complaining, on the contrary smiling – and I am sure keeping mostly to himself the extent of the fears, the distress and the physical unpleasantness – and looking now to doing further writing after this period's enforced slowdown.

David Hart
April 2010

INSIDE OUT-CASTING

Telepathic Relief

You were guiding me from marginal fragments
to the epicentre of dramatic scenes:
from the face of a passer-by
to the accidental audience
where the city square hosted
sunlight in the fountain cascade.

The poem could reduce the white of blankness
from the page as the lines cover
the blank meaning of the sheet itself.

Inside Out-casting

There on the silhouette of this city,
not only the air is bearing
the sign of dusk:

the streetlights cannot turn
their cones upside down
to floodlight the lower sky,

the moss hangs from these street lamps
and expand its shade
but I am missed from that line of green.

There is no division between the evening's
drama and its denouement
in the dark over the hilly outskirts:

the cat's eyes are glowing
between the cars on the motorway
where the noise cannot settle down.

Staring at the moon's capable ascension,
my dog is no longer my companion.
I am left alone in the myth of the earth.

Soon

You tell me, 'See you soon', and you have gone.

Your voice still echoes, every word shredding daylight
as if harpoon after harpoon was flung through
a distillation of unformed tears before the cry.

It still seems the sky took your shadow out of haze,
there is no shade, only the line of nameless trees
where your halo chimes through the breeze.

A pattern of sighs filtering in and out,
your form is airy, far removed from rainbows,
even time is gathered from beyond, from no man's land.

No cloud is alone in the blue, apart from that
of two wings belonging to no bird nor plane in flight,
only the white of an angel appearing in this blank sheet

as I listen still to every sound entering my silence.

Presence

When it was time, you held your doll
and sat on your dad's shoulders
under his umbrella, under that shade of dark.

As he walked through the rain's perpetual tune
chancing your childhood, brightening the grey,
you hummed how the raindrops drummed the black cloth:

tap-tap, tap-tap, the rainwater was fragmented
into separate tones, each drop a note in music,
you closed your ears half on yourself, half on your voice.

it conjured the rhythm of your flight
among the people in the street and you wished
no ending, no landing, no being alone.

Now it's raining again and you feel the sky
could stay over the clouds forever:
harmony expands her hold on daylight

and the day is spread out by its form
while her lover's hand on her shoulder
rejuvenates the membrane of her smile.

Tap-tap, tap-tap, the rainfall cannot reach her
under the transparent bell of her umbrella:
the drummer on her way to the shrine of melody,

she hears the passers-by praising
one who has directed the rainwater concert –
the composer returns to the certainty of her song.

Turning

Before dawn, you gazed at the stars over the horizon
and, seeking sleep amongst thousands of dreams,
you tried to turn stardust into the early sunlight:

*Is it safe to leave your pain not written,
the ache which belongs to your hand
or to stretch out your fingers towards another spring?*

On the garden lawn, the snowman was dying;
how the blankness of your notebook could not be brought
to daylight, the distance finding itself in your diary:

*You've forgotten the night – the damp secret of darkness –
but not the moth caught in the spider web by the door frame
in the corner where the street light is stuck to the dusty wall.*

Nothing like noon mounted the thrashing remnants
of everything invisible, un-gathered and lost for you –
still by the window, your eyes fixed on the bronze sky:

*Who could see the credits of pollen marked on the vase
but not your fingerprints on that glass
empty of water, empty of flowers and as empty as ancient?*

Caressing your reading glasses rather than your pen,
you tried to adopt the power of flight from the wood-pigeon
hoisting its wings above the grey bark of the pine branch:

*Oh girl, clouds also need the air for flying to me –
the afternoon sun sliding from the hammock of the blue;
as if I'm your father, only poetry reaches its destination,*

He said and left the pine bristle between the pages
of the book, each tiny pine leaf
shining like a green filament.

SILENT INHERITANCE

Out of Darkrooms

The lady and the castle-builder
walk along the beach,
a camera hanging around her neck,
his shadow slipping away.

Are you listening to me?
Taking the photograph of a trough,
she cannot hear her own voice
or his reply – *yes, if you are the sea.*

Wave after wave feeds the moats
around the sand castles,
the breeze creeping upon her hair
but not blowing it across the lens.

Are you following the boat?
He paddles in the shallows
and cannot hear himself or her response –
yes, if its sail matches my skirt.

The summer air laces to its frame
in the picture of the low sky:
coping with the sound of water,
the afternoon is their only burden.

Hibernation Cushion

After the sleepless night they are not at ease:
no difficulty in opening their eyes,
no reason to wake up
but they both can see

the fallen tree with its hibernation cushion
of dry leaves not fallen, and spread
beneath the branches on the footpath.

Their grey leaf-skin matches their skeletons
but not the tree surgeons' uniforms:
she gazes at their green shadows
chopping the branches, sawing the trunk;
he stares at the sawdust –
the first sign of the morning's entrance.

Magic Lantern

She is a photographer of happy faces,
her eyes can see
above the surface of objects:

the sails of her images are anchored
in the place alighted on the glitter
rocking in the fluid for processing films.

She is a darkroom magician
who takes photographs of wakened vases
and new flower pots
but roses, blossoms, wild flowers
appear on the white walls of her studio.

The light of her pictures is brighter
than daylight from the sky's cupola:

to benefit from her album-niche
he has to shape his sight less carefully,
so as to collect the scattered details of life.

Celluloid Collection

Overpowered with voices, the evening air
cannot record their contours,
not even they could whisper
to dislodge snow from the evergreen branches.

But the winter hovers its soul-veil
and examines the sound of grass
rising up in their footprints:

be still and draw your smiles,
they teach you how to pose,
it is echoing from their footsteps.

Looking at the reverse of each photograph
they both feel the influence of whiteness –
the twisting path overgrown with flashes.

Non-communicators

No difference between two songs of air:
the air blows through a birdcage
where the bird sings its solitude.

The study furniture witnesses the air
at the address of a double presence –
the stillness of her and the quietness of him.

Although they are not in there
the window looks at them – two absent singers:
they speak no language of things

but the pane talks to them
through its tongue of transparency.

Silent Inheritance

Waiting for the river –
the ultimate mirror that flows
only between two bridges –

to find the balance in the floating jars
of candles on perfumed water.

Listening to the hum of tuning forks,
the song named after
the water's cosmic origins:

to activate the slice of a waterfall
where surface and depth interplay.

Guarding the rainbow from clouds –
the trinket that fades
at the far side of the sky –

to arrive in the waiting-room
before rain melts snow outside.

Removing the Inner-stone

The pebble, stranded by her computer,
cannot be returned to the beach
where it was collected by him:

tonight he still belongs to the dark scene –
the sleepless sea splashes
his hands on her keyboard.

Tonight, sand gathers the summer daylight
as she rolls the shingle
from the seabed to the crests
where the waves' foam-frost is colder
than ice in the crave of the winter's age.

In-earth

Wings on their own cannot fly
despite their sympathy for the skylark
with its thirst for songs and hunger for flocks.

Her hand cannot write on its own
though it, with his other one, bears
a blank sheet through the harmony of a pair.

But her fountain-pen can bleed
if she leaves it uncapped
near an ink-well,

and a feather-duster yet tests the air
on its gravitated fall, as a figurine tries
to break the motionless into movements.

Thanks to the furniture their house is
not empty while they are on holiday:
the hot filaments warm the lampshade,
but not their study.

Thanks to night, dust is hidden in darkness:
if he wants to read her letters,
he has to dig and dig
until light brightens the remnants of envelopes.

Outside the Paradox

As if he is silhouetted against the sail,
her voice dusts down
like plaster-powder coating the shore.

After the waves' return, the beach is
painted in the colour of sand,
yet paint flakes mix with the foam.

The horizon is still a fixed distance
that the sailing boat can leave –
its sails navigated by water ghosts.

Sea wind rattles through the scatter
of tissue shadows in the port
where there are no free moorings.

Air power strips down the call
from the boat, each word –
separate debris prospers along the coast.

Stranded under the branches, she is
the captain of wreckage who cannot escape
the coloured meeting with dusk.

Dream Gap

Night streams through the midsummer
and darkens the fenced enclosure.
Not irritated by the lime tree blossom,
they sleep near the pine tree.

Coloured like the skin of the moon,
the garden is no longer their property,
not even they can tame the sky to enter
and mend their entwined dream.

Clothed only in tree flowers,
passers-by sing and dance in their clogs,
none of them halt to wake the sleepers
to listen to their steps and their song:

we cannot fall asleep and join you
in the base of dying moonlight,
not even our shadows leave
our outstretched arms,
nor can we change
this serenade into
an empty silence.

Kinetic Construction

Abandoned in the open-air dance,
they both blank out
and bear the scars of their souls.

One wreath of grass is still
around their necks,
it remains silently
as it should be in an album.

Lit by the flash reflected
on the ice-surface –
her camera is beneath,
in the frozen flow.

IMPROVISING MEMORY

Today

While they are there,
the evening sun lowers
over woods
but no light can give
its motion to the air.

Passing through the opening
of a window,
only the fire-music comes
from the fire place
and the flower-strewn corpse opposite.

Sitting on the stone bench
near their conservatory
they both are under the pale distance,

the smoke rising from their cigarettes.
The depth of future is
thinner than that of history.

Love Collocation

Watercolours are their failures, constantly.
In contrast, after rain
clouds stay and represent the sky
drawn in pencil.

As they cross a noon-river,
the rainbow, stranded
over the grey horizon,
provides them with its form
of the bridge built of pencil dust.

As they walk from beyond,
there is no water flowing under their feet,
only the scaffolding of shadows
spread over the drawing board.

Exhibitions are their goal, constantly.
In retrospect, after linking
their footsteps, they both learn
how they are always outside,
never in the painting.

Improvising Memory

Ripe fruits fall from the branch
as the orchard fears itself
alone in the autumn avalanche:
        the quince could not stain grass,
        its new home beneath the tree.

In the house full of reflecting objects
only the tongue of a grandfather clock
moans for the past:
        as no-one throws earth into a grave,
        the echo grows from a coffin.

Whoever consumes air now
between the farm and the graveyard
ruins the arch of stillness:
        no-one comes to this empty room
        and gathers the quince's smell
        by the fruit basket.

No Difference

To re-enter an olive grove
she needs insouciance, not a gate
to pass through, to experience
the minutiae of water –
the surface of a rainbow over the trees.

To pick up a dandelion clock, not ruining
the cult figure of the afternoon silence,
he has no need for a conceptual peacefulness:

between the gate and the lane
grass is more certain than green colour –
their failures are optional,
repetitions are compulsory.

Beyond the Singer

Adding colours to the flower pots
she builds the vertical surfaces
against the wall:
        late is too late to recognise
        that her love exists
        only in the letters covered
        by his straw hat.

With the patience of clouds
she waters his obsessive memory
on the window-sill:
        passing, blurred as burnt summer,
        noon notices the dark corners
        through the half-opened door
        but not him on the terrace.

There is no music, no song
of walking on waves
along the fatal shore:
        the inky sky falls
        onto the accordion remembrance
        of his envelopes,
        he still sings about her biography.

Hermitage

Surrounded by half-darkness,
the lampshade protects two moths
flying around the bulb:
>if she turns off the light,
>the insects will not be silhouetted
>against the illusion-cone
>at the furthermost end of the evening.

If he can harmonise the music
of his mouth-organ with the wings,
the illusory space could
be turned into a dance hall:
>inherited with no talent
>for blowing air,
>he prefers the imminent silence
>of no motion.

Blended together, the signal
from her watch and the sound
from the tower clock
belong to time immemorial:
>the night has many drawbacks
>in its hermetically-sealed endurance.

At zero visibility outdoors, neither stardust
nor moonlight can emigrate
to the local colour of indoors:
>since he obstinately refused
>to write dancing-music,
>there is no companion
>who could work a duet
>and read the notation for tomorrow.

Tomorrow

There are no keys to open
the indoors – the place
where he had asked his love out.

There is no coach to pass
through the gate
of the airy countryside ruins.

But it is possible to replace
the plot of scenery: nothing is
missing from the view of an agony.

In her last sleep,
the previous evening becomes the first
to the ending of her morning dream.

Darkness fills his eyes up to their brim,
as, in the outline of a niche,
he sees someone else instead of himself.

A new day is hiding again:
a warm message rhymes
with their long marriage.

Two Pretenders

The swan surrounded by a thin ice-layer
in the pond, trying to climb
onto the frozen surface, struggles.

Oh, how careless you are.
Your slice of bread is out
of the bird's reach, the icy water speaks
to the couple in the park.

Winter in their hearts grows
away from their bodies,
as the flock of flashbacks land
on the frost-field of their memories.

You are only there to feed
the migratory guest
in the city, but not able
to decipher the codes of the attempt.

The ice is their lecturer of the season.
But looking at the pale scene
they see only the plot of lilies.

Love's Enthusiast

He was an enthusiast whose eyes were
blinking between either open
or closed perspectives:
he was taking a photo of her
who knew nothing about his love.

Leaning against a tree and, nearly unnoticed,
he held his disposable camera
as long as a moment could be
expanded in a ten-minute stretch.

It was a festival colouring a park,
he attended her family picnic
under the parasol which, with its shadow,
had made the grass greener.

In the middle of the summer,
the grass was ironed by her family members
and saved from the sunshine
beaming from the sky.

From the view of the garden hedge
their touch belonged
to the afternoon shade like a kiss, hidden

in their silhouettes passing through dusk –
their arms greeted each other
by waving to the evening light.

Escaping Emptiness

A gap between two rainbows
is bridged by colouring life-lines:
> a face cannot react
> with other faces
> lacking harmony
> when a smile abandons it.

An opening in the midwinter storm
is measurable by snow:
> a heart cannot receive
> an avalanche of mountain air
> nor do flakes shed
> their whiteness and cold into it.

An empty space between two dreams
is not noticeable in the eyes of night:
> stars disappear beyond sight
> not showing their ripeness
> leaving the moon –
> rotten fruit of the pale sky.

Entitled

A gaping hollow of a letter-box
never reachable by frost:
> leaves of early sunshine
> slide down the roof slope
> to ruin grass crystals –

the hand of morning warming the ground.

A wait between two birthdays,
there is another year
to blow away:
> an infinity of flames may
> strengthen candles
> into the fire that flags

from the glow of burning birthday cards.

FUTURE FORGOTTEN

Guidance

A darkroom restorer builds
the complete picture of an ancient beacon:
when crossing to the other side
her eyes are the only ground that people need.

  A skeleton of tenderness could be
  used as a guide for self-sacrifice:
  it is time to save a panorama
  and not spoil the flight with another feather.

A trail of ash footprints is turned
into the sure way to an iconic fireplace:
when passing through the hearth
her breaths join the unfinished chain of air.

  A south wind blows only quiet birdsongs
  from the weather-vane on a rock:
  her new experience fits the rhythm sensed
  by memories of sharing warmth with summer.

Picture Study

This was no album to be treasured.

Two wine glasses, half-full in the mirror
but empty on the table –
one reflected red,
the other one eroded by changeless air.

There is a dreamer – acting
on the stage of her living room:

a part of silence, framed for someone,
pressing her portrait to the wall –
her hand with a cigarette,
motionless, suspended by the rising smoke.

She goes under the skin of another failure
and has to be a statue bearing
the immeasurable layer of black paint:

stuck in the eddy of the air-pocket,
her breath retains
the origins of its outdoor forms.

Petrified Duet

Pressed against the window
a plant faces sunlight
        but fades:
        no escape
from the dry soil –
        the promised land
of the green-coloured flower-pot.

Autumn has aroused skinless pain.
He measures pauses
        between his breath:
        smoke from
the burnt birch-bark mould
        matches the grey-blue line
            from his pipe.

Air delivers reality by the tone
of afternoon and acquaints
        two home companions:
        he avoids his memory
of the gift-bearing
        that reflects only
granite indifference.

Through the Media of a Moment

Water cools her shadow
in the pond –
the tender place undisturbed
      by the pouring
      paint of sunshine
but by a watering-can in her hand.

No words to rescue their house
of poured-out silence
      from the dark-pale leaves:
      another gravity is
halfway between them –
      outdoor-indoor
blendings are open wide.

Into the Reflection

The camera flash reflected
in the mirror: *who wanted
to preserve that image of a utopian acre?*

Night's tidal wave of darkness surrounds
both glass edges: the form cannot
escape from the looking-glass –
love remains as it was, is and will be.

Visionaries sight a path along summer fields
to the place of their own: to ignore
the speed of the half-moon gondola
leaves her eyes deep.

Blinkered, seizing the logic dusk:
a lamp in the skeleton of a little wooden boat
is re-imagined not remembered – lost air
escorting them to the collection of kiss-keys.

Spirit Maturation

On the roof, footprints
are what they were –
the signs of an interactive arrival:

innocent of old proverbs,
a tree-conserver has warmed
her feet on the solar slates.

That house behind sunset
cannot face nightfall, the air is
isolated from the cold evening:
every step depends on light,
the sky above that pathway quivers.

The grammar of her pace
marks the season's sense of itself:
no shadow is dead and compiled –
the silhouette indicates
an indigo backdrop.

As quiet as a meadow stream,
she draws the curtains
of her consciousness:
heaven's edge nearby teaches
only how to get her face out of a hood.

Attachment

Covered with a love-veil
an awakening grows:
>no avoidance of a poplar
>from the garden's outline.

An interplay between dawn stars
limits the sky in debris of sleep:
>the pale-yellow of autumn gathers
>in dream-light around the tree.

Air fuels the view of an open window:
the replica of a house, an alarm-clock,
>each acts in one-way direction –
>no border between amnesia and memory.

Future Forgotten

In front of the florists
he could not enlarge
          the flowers' tears –
rain poured into her embrace,
          water filled
his sleeves and pockets.

Later on in her home
at the burial address:
          air dried his clothes
wind shut the window
its frame cut the flowers,
          petals discarded inside,
the pieces of a vase outside.

Today, sunlight is still ancient
but the woman's heart
          is not at ease:
the blackbird lands on a yew tree –
          only her garden knows
why the dark feathers
          match the deep green.

Observation Window

Between rain they watch a plot of land
overlooked by the angels:
                        a grass sonata
is disturbed by pickaxes
delving in the rhythm of wise blood –
                        inch by inch, earth
becomes less wild beneath.

Through green against the dark soil,
drawings and plans translate
                        into foundation stones:
a chain of harmony
carries the most valuable house-seeds –
                        side by side
their potential selves are packed together.

Sunlight deludes them
into the homeless shadows
                        mixed with silence.
The air is their second skin:
                        as real as stars
at the collapse of noon,
scissors and window-frames are made
                        of the same eternal origami.

Trees are the stuff of fantasy
in a paper street
                        and the sky searches
the interior of the dome
as a bird sings from a picture
                        not from a cage.
This day is removed
to an illusory address –
                        they both are the architects
imprisoned in their only building.

Grasping for the Surface

Between eyes and mirrors
>there are no reborn flowers
>but the double silhouettes –
>>his and hers,
>the host and her guest
in the palace monologue of self.

Between distances and outlines
>there is a flower stall
>certain as sunset:
>>in her inescapable hug
>she dreams the mystery of wings
as the evening has come without its dusk.

Between the walls of inexhaustible paintings
>in the gallery of non-shadows
>there is an embrace:
>>his hands guide her through
>the naive style of love,
they are drawn into the paint of their skin.

Degree of Vacuum

Going to sleep they leave
the sky overloaded
with leaf-like kites, not with stars:

their hammock is closer
to the earthy ground
than the dreams stretched between two trees.

Falling asleep does not carry them
to space but separates
them from other people:

their dreams, unprotected on the summer bed,
fade quicker than a book-cover
exposed to the afternoon sunshine.

They are not afraid of that bedroom
in the open air
but of awakening too late:

the small garden fountain cannot
pretend to be their friend
but water from its cascade is their alarm-clock.

Dual Projection

Looking at the rainbow
through her sunglasses,
it is someone else
who ignores what these words are for –
their letters are like petals folded back.

Watching the flock of swans
in their flight behind the clouds,
she uses a pair of binoculars:
someone else discovers again
through her eyes where south ebbs.

Listening to the skylark's song
from the oak at the field's edge,
she is part of the blurred fiction:
someone from the suspended morning
settles reality instead of the bird.

FINDING DARKROOM PRINTS

The Imprint of Three Seconds

Why I squeeze the ink out of my pen?

But the sound of earth is louder
and he hears only it sliding
from the wheelbarrow into a flower-grave.

She, who has buried
a huge pile of fallen flower petals,
puts on her black veil to mourn in their garden.

As he pushes a wheel-rim
from the patio floor to the footpath,
she has no care for the dominos
leaning upon each other and falling
into water from the fountain edge.

But the ghost of a sheet
is faceless and able to pass
their hands to the earth
before the view of sunset begins
to dive at dusk.

Tepid Support

Yesterday, today, tomorrow –
what is next to spare
their vision of the butterfly
swinging on the cotton of the butterfly net?

Something from past, something from future,
as she tosses the laurel leaf
into a bowl filled with dew
or into a basin of melted frost.

Violin, mandolin, tambourine,
three out of millions of tears
belong to the mountain of clouds,
not to those on the artist's hill.

Sometimes soul, sometimes spirit
comes to play the strings
of kites flying and migrates
from nearness to the wreath of his amnesia.

Shadows are useless without light –
it is how to eclipse the scores
in the forest
of their fog-wounded fingers.

Blossom Rain

Rain stopped but the weather forecast
has no information for them:
clouds are gathered for a funeral
as the family chooses a coffin –

the wood with white velvet blossoming.
The spirit appears to be the air,
not conjured but sifted
through the curtain to meet them:

dusk begins to caress the tree flowers –
the only proof of their non-existence.
The grave is so full of horizon lines
that have lost their unreachable forms,

the blue peeled from the sky's roof.
The colour of night is alike
any painter's liquid – it never fades
despite stars closer than every afterlife.

Joined-up Writing

The nightwear folded on a bed
and the note with the marks
of his finger-bones jointly bear silence.

Frost peels birches outdoors,
as he journeys by his hand –
the ink-thread tracks the changes of address.

Recycling moonlight is set
to the letter of bloodlines in an envelope,
the silence runs among the cold interior.

Ash has lost its warmth,
the fire-place knows of other flames
where he can lay his breath.

Tethered to Home

The window's vertical pane
bears a feeder sealed on it
but the glass also is
a mirror set in concrete
for a robin eating hazelnuts.

And yet the window is
the soul of his pottery studio:
looking through the inside of himself
he softens the bird –
the clay flying between his hands.

At the morning's turn into daylight
the red wings of the air bring
the outdoors to him:
brought at the fading moment,
the woe between his lips remains
like a last supper for the artist dwindling.

Now

No certainty in his steps
as he streams
to find a wellspring,
parallel with a brook, the ground
bears only the speed of water.

As he walks upstream,
'now' is never the adverb
of past-time, but two equals two
while two handfuls of clay
slide into his pockets.

At the destination of impossible,
from the view of the source,
everything is downstream:
the clay is still in the two spaces
reserved for his gloves.

Fading Darkroom Prints

In the square for people and monuments
it is a wonder between her
and his camera –
their passion for pictures
against the nature of things.

Standing next to the fountain well
they examine the memory
of themselves:

each flashback tosses stealthily,
each circle enlarges its volume
and extends itself
out of water and grows further
around the stony ground.

As the lenses duel with the fact
of a non-afternoon,
she beholds that fight
between the human and the object
but he loses the brightness of his smile.

Runners from Each Other

He is colour-blind if he meets
the breeze that had ruffled
his long brown hair:

in fact it will be the reverse –
the air could caress
his short grey hair at his blind date.

Mapping his home,
his love has no foothold there,
and there is not a piano to play

the music of fragments of always:
he is a piano tuner, his tears cannot
be distilled, salt burdens them.

He returns to the house of double hearts
and sees them both ways
as he crosses lines of the isolated afternoon.

His mouth is interred, his lips buried
into the broad outdoors, none of his fingers
try to run and beat the pistol-kiss.

Rebuilding Warmth

There are three layers of cold
in his shirt pocket:
the sharpness of snow,
of ice
and that of frost upon his chest,
as she is not with him
on the route along the canal.

There are three ways of cutting veins,
not leaving a scar:
the bitterness
of a frozen razor,
of his pale fingers
and that of his coagulated shadow
which tenders his slow pace.

Only water accompanies him –
the scaffolding of his clothes
in the winter chill.

Destined

They cannot lean against the fallen tree
nor can they search for strength
to prop it.

The fatal air supports only their shadows
stretched near each other –
two different forms
but united in the shade
of the same winter's green.

As if they could hover in the acre
of the sky above the pruned trunk
that leans upon the ground,
the tree is able to join itself
with the branch-like mark:

the ghost of what once belonged to the tree,
the ghost of dark soil,
leaf-mould and yellowed grass.

DOUBLE IDENTITY

Non-composure

Night follows day not vice-versa,
words tread on the lines of a poem:
love is passing the fossil
of his age, of his breaths.

Sleep comes behind a bedtime song,
dreams are not insomnia images:
his voice grows through flames of powder
but dusts over his bed full of lichen.

Dawn appears after the music
played by his alarm-clock,
its tune and rhythm are too fast
for writing in slow motion.

Morning arrives through the curtain –
the sail on the boat of daylight:
he departs from the bed-linen
in the numbed skin-coffin of his body.

Crestfallen Diver

Caught beneath the ice of a lake,
the underwater bird cannot
break the surface of the winter cage.

In the water-setting it is warmer
than frost on her pendant –
the crystal design of her necklace.

The bird cannot sing any song
to make her feel the outdoor concert,
the ripples in the ice – a gramophone record.

There are two alphabets to be read:
first – she handles her love-shield
and protects it from absorbing the cold,

second – she prefers feathers
in flight
to the scene of the folded wings.

Double Identity

As he opens the window, the dove
takes off from the sill;
the air embraces its feathers
rather than his thought of the flower.

The sky again won
through the bird leaving the view
of his blindness:
his illusion fades
as the evidence of her becomes real –
sharp, fresh water
that he has poured
into an empty flower pot.

But she is not the water
and it is not her:
it has the blue
from between two clouds,
the water is gentle
and blue as his eyes once were.

The water is a drink
for his abandoned wing-friend
which is flying thirsty and free
not sharing its flight
with the evident flower, she.

Two Figures

Not the bird in its cage
but the love-song still haunts her:
each breath struggles –
melting the snowflake
of his kiss on her lip.

Even the word *never* appears
to be made from ice –
the frozen feather
like a hand-wave flies
over the iron fence:
Is your hand yours
as you wave from the park?

Though he is a birdwatcher
he cannot listen to the bird's notes:
Iron is iron as cold is cold,
two sides of the iron are
the same colour of cold.

The gate bars are painted
in green from his side,
in yellow-brownish from hers,
and the sliding gate is still between them.

Pining for a Close-up

A pot filled with tea for two
is served for them.
He waits for her to share
their drink.

The vapour passes
through the hole in a lid
and weaves his gaze:
distance belongs to her as always.

The heart-like piece of moss decorates
the pine table arranged
for the love occasion:
two serviettes,
folded at the same time for them,
will not be used
nor two tea bags anchored
as one in the hot water.

With nearly perfect synchronization
time guides him
both to past and future,
nothing of him remains
apart from his sigh above the tablecloth.

Two Hurts

Three skin-masks cover her face
as she flirts with the single flower
in a thin narrow vase –
the rose of her heart
blossoming in the middle of February.

Three ice cubes wait to be thawed
by juice in the glass
but his cold hand stops melting –
each cube reflects
the fragments of her figure.

One candle flame-eye glows
between the two groups
of the threes:
it is his eye –
the inner burning mirror
where her eyes grow
filled with thorns.

The cut rose will never wilt
between the meat of her partner's lips.

Not an Interpolation

One square of a tablecloth is
enough to be a stage
for the cigarette dying
on the brim of an ashtray.

The fading glow releases smoke:
the grey thread sews the trapeze
for his breath
for his tribute to the magic of love.

Over the porcelain rim my fingers
are not what they are,
she examines her heartbeats
through the nature of visibility.

He listens to her – the ice-drinker
whose voice sifts
snow dust and frost dust –
two parts of the latent act.

Variant Evidence

He loses a tool for digging stars
from graves all over the sky
as sunlight covers the morning silence.

In the repentant mural of time,
the river rhymes with water,
its double hydrogen not able

to escape the presence of air
while a vase sets free the flowers
from the porcelain design.

The shadow of his rocking chair
moves across the verandah wall,
it cannot represent
a static moment in the painting

through the handful of dew
while the earth in the flower pot
waits to be watered by his hands –
the two variations of the same ink.

Mourner's Tribute

The line of willows waits for the stream,
not she.
Water flows in free verse
downstream and away.

Sunshine obeys the laws of sky –
obedient to the bridge,
the shadowy stone arches are
formless, not she.

The colour of mourning exposes
the departure of leaves
from the trees:
they sail, not she.

He cannot recognise
sunlight floating
more in the whirlpools,
less on the fallen leaves.

The early evening sun lights
his breath in the air
as it flows from him –
he is not able to step out from his body.

Expiry

At Christmas time the hyacinth was
in flower: from its pot
the scent reached the tiny fire flames
flickering through the air
between the partners.

They both felt the comfort
of two palm-readers: their hands able
to tell what they can hold
if the future appears
drawn like a palisade on a palette.

At Valentine time the hyacinth came
out of bloom: she replaced it
with her partner's roses,
the vase overgrown by their blossom.

His gift taken outdoors:
his heart no longer had
any real influence
over the colour of their brick patio.

Frost ingratiated itself with the garden,
frost ingrown inwards into his skin.

Dancing Music

The birch mourns for its bark
as she believes that the tree
poses before her evergreen camera.

He, like a deciduous guest,
welcomes daisies
growing around the tree trunk.

Dew from the branches
waters down his wine
and dances in traces in his glass.

From her smile the sun disperses
the filaments of its bliss,
her eyes harbour a shadow for safety.

Only daydreams can bring her
back to the sunshine,
its dance steps in the rhythm of the leaves.

BLANKETED

Late Honeymoon

The fire eats a book of poetry.
Their meal will be served
just before the cold ashes
pile themselves in the fire-place.

Dancing with two armfuls of sea-water
they leave the late evening,
their footprints lead them
from the kaleidoscope
of memory to the house of reality.

Their footsteps guide them to the end
of their honeymoon dance:
nothing can go backwards
apart from the midwinter.

Moonlight follows them
and passes through the door
they have not closed,
their shadows absorb
the warm air of the tourist resort.

Crossover

At the leave of a bridge
water remains
uncrossed for the reflections
floating upstream;
with some dry clay
he returns to his pottery studio.

Within a waiting distance,
he touches his wheel;
his pots are positioned
at intervals on the shelves
but there is no connection
between the clay bags.

Sleep Advantage

In her dream, the perspective
of a camera swings
like a pendulum
but she sees the flash-sails
in the winter wind.

The tripod stand is stranded in the pond
filled with the leaf-skeletons,
each has a dark pupil
belonging to her.

After the dream,
night is still between two days:
there are two daylights –
yesterday's and tomorrow's metaphor
of the utopia reality cannot
substitute for poetic justice.

She is still balancing
on the scales of a secret-land.

Synchronicity

Differentiating between before,
now and later,
they blend daylight with flash
as her camera follows the rhythm
of a wedding dance.

Music directs the bride and her groom
between the piano crescendo
and the violin's song:
their steps bring no shadows
but accelerate the present out of itself.

Collecting remnants into the sum
of nearness,
she steals the moment.
It may be converted into pictures
in a future-album.

The newly married ignore
the indolence of the day.
As the plants sense the dancers,
their leaves are open
both to beauty and harmony.

Silver Winter

Two waves meeting each other
near the ship leaving a port.

Before they mix their foam,
before the lighthouse begins
to mark the distant island
like a watercolour on paper,
they walk along the quay under snow.

The snow on their clothes is not
part of nature any more.

Before it loses its whiteness,
before they return
to their home atmosphere,
on his own he searches for a glow
in the line of their melted footprints.

As dusk darkens the afternoon's paint,
they are less alone
among the lit street lamps.

The ship has departed the horizon
and passed night to the town.

Before the sea quietens down,
before the footprints completely stamp
the white carpet broadened
at the quayside,

they take part in the race of the silver winter.
Still waving from the bow,
she is in the lead.

Slower are the clouds
streaming opposite,
even slower are the waves
arriving in pairs,
the slowest is he –
he at the end of his breath.

Continuity

Influenced by the sea
they walked and endured
the evening along the beach.

The night air blanketed
their silhouettes,
the tidal layer could not
cover their footprints.

Now in the shallows,
their footprints are still on water:
abandoned they float,
not even remains of sand are sunken.

At noon he will return
to collect these marks
for the future strolls with her.

Holiday House

Wind, a door and a shadow:
the wind opens the door
and flies into the porch
but the shadow remains outside.

With the air trapped inside
now the returner is locked –
the photograph of a traveller
on a boat in a bottle.

The sea cannot reach the doorstep:
water develops itself
from the negative to the picture
of a glass-blower on the beach.

Still

Behind the oars
two tracks in the sand
of the beach
that lead to a boat –
the paper boat in the shallows.

Burdened with foam
waves run unstoppable
run to the ending
of their journey.
The summer remains where it was.

Hunter

Between two birds in flight
lies only
the responsibility for dreams –
his ice-arrow fired
through the colours of a breeze
to the safety of the sky.

Between the tracks of a sledge
are only his footprints
in the snow spread
from this moment to the future perfect –
time marked by the pattern of his pace
towards a utopian calendar.

Anti-burial

Church bells are ringing, ringing –
the sounding of iron from the belfry:
music that teaches
how to cross without dying
the boundaries between
birthdays and afterlife.

As if she dances with loved ones
and for the flames on candles,
she familiarises herself
with the neutral ground
where she can decipher noon
in the praise of the shadows buried in things.

Blanketed

In his linen-tent he has no sleep:
in the room, darkness is suited
to the veils of air tied between the walls.
From his hand the torchlight sweeps
along the photograph of a corn field
where cicadas' song deepens the summer.

Covered with his blanket, he sits on the bed:
already torn many years ago,
the picture of the poem-bearer in the lane cannot
be healed by the cone of light;
although he is near the wheat field
the music reaches miles away but not him.

And no need for glue to mend
the image of him daydreaming
on the branch split from its tree:
filled with darkroom prints,
his album endures the length of the night.

EDITING THE SILENCE FROM THE PHOTOGRAPHS

Inconsistent

To cast the spindrift of leaves
in the morning layered
by the blank air,

I linger around the tree and serve
the fall-in-reverse under the branches
escaping from their essential bareness.

To advance on the words
further than in breathing
by my search for oxygen,

I collect tissues of the misty veil,
all that grief condensed
in the inheritance of this ephemeral whiteness.

To handle the mist
that forces its way upward
from my hold,

I examine the recurrent daylight
through the notion of what poetry is –
a tune from the hollow bone.

Retaining

Something shook you awake to the now of March
as you were assigned to the morning –
the dream which has ceased to expire:

*crocuses – white, purple and yellow – are
flowering in the grass, scanned by daylight
on the island between two busy roads,*

*destined to become forgotten.
The floral tribute laid a month ago – now it is
a blur of decay on the pavement opposite.*

The shadow from the dry side of the window
cannot hide the identity of your bedroom –
the place where none but the sun can match itself:

*there, the accident happened in February
when the car knocked down the snowman
where he stood in the central reservation*

*and the bench is still marked with a rash of lichens
where his builder used to play and sing like birdsong
of the blackbird taken from the snowman's heart.*

Someone could set you free from your sleep
as if the surface of your memory
would vibrate while ashes burst into fire:

*there, before the tragedy near the churchyard,
only the street light could change its angle
when the car followed the night air as it lengthened*

*the tyre tracks, darkened the layer of snow,
as she witnessed by the curtains, drawn
to its openness and up to her touch.*

Now you can retrace the plastic flowers fading
and arising from the disillusionment, the sunlight
leaves by stealth from the end to the beginning again.

Rorschach Test

Your writing is made up of music
with a blank dot at the end of the stave,
you play your fountain-pen – your flute
releases the air in the pattern of sound
while you reveal what a mountain can reach,

touching the inky sky: *Take my breath –*
your compass for the untitled evening concert –
and dance with your fingers across the flute.
Each fingertip in its place, each can search
for the coordinates of a classical minuet.

As if a butterfly is flying to the florists
and leads me to find a spray of roses for you –
a musician bowing from the symphony stage,
I hold the butterfly wings – the essence
of a metaphor fading in the palm of my hand,

exposed to the street lamp: *Go back to the garden*
where you cut the flowers from their green cradles
and let the butterfly follow you on your return
to the meadow where a still life never does exist
and listen to the major keys of the vacuum.

If this test is folded in half and laid on the stand,
the image is divided into the silence that counts –
the interval between the past and the future,
echoing the poem from the paper,
the act of prevailing.